The Four Colors

The Four Colors

Ankur

HAWAKAL

hawakal

Published by Hawakal Publishers
185 Kali Temple Road, Nimta, Kolkata 700049
India

Email info@hawakal.com
Website www.hawakal.com

First edition July, 2020

Cover image: Shutterstock
Cover design: Bitan Chakraborty

ISBN: 978-81-945273-2-9

Price: 350 INR | USD 9.99

To
Manju

without her
the universe wouldn't exist

CONTENTS

GREEN

YELLOW

PURPLE

RED

Introduction

It has been many years since poetry first came to me: fitfully as a child and in an irresistible flow as I became a young man. This process of accretion has left deposited several layers of thought and imagination and memories and dreams: there are dreams, or rather fragments of them, that have stayed and have become memories, and there are memories that have become dreamlike, that do not seem real anymore. Most of these memories and dreams consist of a particular way the breeze blew and how it smelt in a particular place and time, the gleam with which heavy raindrops bounced on tarmac roads on monsoon nights under sodium vapor lamps, the fascinating soft light from a bedside lamp that shined alone in the night as others slept. Such ensconced images in all of us give meaning to our existence, and even if my particular memory may be different from yours, my evoking of one may evoke another for you: it is thus that without you knowing me and me knowing you, we still can know each other well.

The poems in this slim volume were written by me over the course of several years, most of them under the duress of intense emotion. They all reflect a certain color of life, a certain phase of our existence: green as it relates to birth, curiosity, ambition; the yellow encountered, as in disillusion in the face of injustice, anger, listlessness, fear, and then in trying to make sense of the world around us; a purple, when we dare to reopen to the world, leading to a rebirth, with attendant wonder, dreams, fantasies, as we become ready to love anew; and red when we start understanding and accepting, as simultaneously we find acceptance and love. These are not necessarily neat compartments: just as colors themselves do not exist solely in their stark purity, so do the parts of our lives often segue into each other with no clearly defined hue or moment. In a way, they represent a certain linearity, for we aim to understand ourselves, to be our own masters as we grow, and they also represent a certain circularity, for we cycle constantly among these, without a defined chronology, as we try to avoid being stationary. This we call *life*.

My fervent wish as a poet is that reading these poems evokes poetry in you too.

This book wouldn't have got completed without the unwavering support of my mother, father and my wife as well as the rest of my family and friends. It still mightn't have seen the light of the day if not for the publishing team at *Hawakal*.

Ankur
Norway

How will I fight and stay,
How will I be silent but remain understood,

How will I speak and not be labelled,
How will I stay still but move,

How will I believe and not be questioned,
How will I question but not shake faith,

How will I be beautiful and yet be,
How will I soar high up but never be far,

How will I love and forget contempt,
How will I do what I am born for, but welcome death always,

How will I die but waft out like perfume,
How will I know Him in every act, just or unjust,

How will I arrange the flowers so every tear gets his due,
How will I wither and wilt, so only spring is remarked,

How will I laugh purely, with no whys tagged,
How will I be a madman but not caged,

How will I change forms but with not a grain of past,
How will I see yet myself through the myriad shapes,

How will I tell them, the poet needs love, and little else,
How will I find a worthy heart, not a fine ear?

GREEN

mother, I

In the bowl of milk and prunes, there are many suns.
Morning comes and goes, but that hand keeps moving;
lips know it, and a soul is nourished.

Pray For Me, Or Not

From one star
I weave to another star
like drawing candles.
Big blue slate
is the world of citylights,
a wind whispers and here is one flicker gone.
A door shuts somewhere, frozen butterflies
in the spreading honey,
the warmth oozing from muffled throats.
Soon the sun shines
and tumbles me out of bed, life already started
and blood flowing, flowing. In spurts and rills.

Sun In The Life

Small boats of paper–
afloat gingerly, what's beyond the rim?
No storms exist in the puddle,
I will remain crouched, unsatiated,
thrilled with that dream–
paper, that came from my notebook,
can also make ships,
that discover worlds, embark on stories.

Survival

Time has erased
wild desires of poetry,
the great boulders lie strewn about
where once the river gushed, of love and song.

The dried ravines, though
are not a bit less beautiful,
for there now walk their bicycles a boy, a girl,
slowly forging ahead, to discover the world anew.

They who only know sweet pomegranates,
can still dream of a moon-lashed sun, and better,
of bobbing umbrellas under a kind drizzle,
can still converse with eyes of curiosity
even if their voices be now muted.

Here walk the last denizens,
behind them is none but a horde of mobs,
but they are hoarse, they are far,
aye, quite far to they who don't hear, only listen.

For listen to the plick-plock, the drip-drop
while from wounded hearts a new stream is squeezed
that might still wound an unminding canyon
through upheavals of dust, fossilised capacities.

As I say, while the two live, new rivers shall flow.

In The Botanical Garden

I went from park to bench,
and I found no fruit hanging,
no person standing,
I saw around the misty enclosure,
there were stabs of rain,
and a whiplashed tumble of kids
on the soft lawn,
and I found no glance waiting,
no leaf quivering;
for the final absolution I walked
to the terraced greenery, a host
of ornamentals basked in patterned laughter;
a last worm trying to eat grass
was my finality, and I left no one waiting
no one to return.

Iron, Iron...

Seasalt, I gather, hands running on the old gate
the sound of ocean booming not far, always in the ear
always loud, crashing. Renting the air. The house in limbo,
the crows sitting on the rooftop suspended, the wires
dangling as if lightning will strike them any time. Smell,

the kind I hate in books. But I love in seasand,
it is here, everywhere; even the windows
eyes of the woman who plays piano on the upper storey
has it, like the entrails of mollusks. Seventy
men may march in and light a fire, yet doesn't go away.

Rocks, the ones we hear seawaves lash to, they feel
black, porous, they feel amphibians; they are an alien creature
their permeable souls keep retaining the weather,
but not the mood,
so the sky, the gulls, the boys who come to bathe,
the lovers for privacy
they can be victims of water, shapeless.

I rasp the rust in my hands, and listen to the old noises,
the wind from coast running high, a woman wailing,
a man guffawing;
I look up at the stars hidden by those gables,
look up more at the fading sky

and see the relief-lit window: green sofa,
red lampshade, something in wait
the woman rubbing a vase, listening to steps.
Footsteps of the hue she knows.

As it grows cold and dark and only bones shiver,
a piano fights against the seascape.

Runningaway

I cut the apple in 2.
Spilt worms, bleeding. Like red latch
of my door. It also creaks.
She brought the terrine, it was seemed
hot. I let fly the windows open,
and moths and dust streamed in. The sunlight
had suffused long ago the walls' pallor,
now paints stared from valueless faces.
I twirled the screwdriver; to horror
there were caterpillars rummaging my brain.
Gnash, and gnash, and wham, the bureau
of iron and steel strong, now ticked
with the timepiece on its top, matching
heart's rhythm. Till the day shuts in,
blinds are drawn. Then, only a lonely
walk in the grass outside; and final blue clouds.

A Change Of Scenery

Among newspapers and hospitable sofas,
I have been busy and bored,
I do not walk anymore in heavy mists under a red sun
Nor tap umbrella onto the floor for dancing with it.
The plains of dust, fed by rivers of silt
where messengers fanned out on horses with gold
are long vanished,
for I feel a different me, neither healthy, nor sick,
but only trying to sustain youth against my wayward tricks.
But change is no worse or better, only if I understand it,
for now I travel among vales of sweet white flowers,
where colours are few but intense, splotched across the sky and sea,
and there may not be horsemen under the tree shade anymore
but pervades the sweet scent of pine, the sweeter of acceptance,
for camphor may not grow everywhere, but smells so brightly
as to inhabit the mind for ever,
giving an unknown company to the mountain airs.

As Night Comes, The Colors Drip, Come Alive

Often as I walk the brown washes away
in the swirling raindust, in the eyes of men watching with envy
in a horizon that is limpid,
where men light-jacketed walk and walk, with earphones
coffee cups, lakeside villas, the teeth of him fond of tobacco
and as it does, I step on the brown dog's tail: the bite, the yelp,
the guilt.

On days of sun and tarmac though, it is the blue that fades
into awnings of ice cream people, the transport endless
of the day's wishes the year's residue; the hairdressers,
the executives, the RJs; a funfair of give-and-take, search-look;
and as I walk, a shout hails me from a theater; munching tomato
sandwiches, the jarring.

Going Up The Skips

High to the shelves made of mango trees, the heat is piled up,
and a warm sky trembles with a love hidden,
a knife drawn from clasp–the words of sweetness, the act of devilry.
Four plums I shall dream of, a good and even number,
that can be divided,
the fog and the winter's hands shall taste them first, make the cross
of truth and the sign of prayer on them; there,
a heavy voice will fall, a girl will cry; there,
the scenes will be played
for a hundred days–then,
the rains shall come, then there shall be a jolly laugh.

An Autumn Storm

Sometimes I see sewn clouds
floating chained in the firmament,
not knowing if they ought to break loose
give scattered showers with gaping holes in between,
or make a storm that spares no life
except a poet's lonely words
burst forth in outraged self-absorption.

YELLOW

Pinning A Butterfly

A last flutter
and there the wings die–
the boy's laugh pleases the mother.

An eye ferocious
unveiled as oranges stray,
the dust storm will hide.

Tanks roll
and houses are searched–
They scan their bodies.

He slaps her
routine
the child whines for rattle.

This time perfume–
the capacity pleases her,
the musicians sing.

The scissor snips
as fragrance is carried home–
to wait for the next day's dead.

Beer and swagger
and soon the day lost in burp–
life with hot afternoons.

Untitled

a simple four-leaved flower
a white that is pale, but still reminds of snow
and a thin glass stem to hold it, like
a murder arrested, as if one has walked into frozenness
and no one else moves, keep walking.

The Sinking Bob Of Cork

From between the stone slabs grew plants,
a dancing checkerboard made its own face;
the evening-fall brings its own prayer with it
where outside only bells toll, a flock returns,
and they eat with noise. stones stuck in gullet.

The afternoon was hot, the cool floor now
brings more hurt to the worn legs, worn body,
before soon night will fall, and there will be
only glow worms shining outside. The remaining
attend to the music for the dead.

Go Stand In One

Open the rose,
peel the petals one by one,
how does it taste? Good?
Slice it, slither it in little rolls,
suck it, and now again taste it.
How does it taste, good?
Good. Now start with another rose.

Often the door opens, and I stand staring
into the stairway, where light comes in little holes;
I stand, feeling no one, but the wind blows across me,
lets me know the earth and the corners of the earth
where you may stand, where I may stand.

The corners where we stand
were those Magellan could not find, nor Stanley,
the places where the disease never struck,
where white thought could not find its way, neither the will;
the place where we climb to blue peaks shining purely,
where intrigue is in the battle of rain and sun, and not the words,
nor the hearts; the place where mirror
does not stand for the image, but the sky.

No, I don't speak white, and I don't speak black.
It will be easy to prove sense as nonsense,
because we already have decided there's no absolute;

it is easy to kill, for life is worthless,
and conscience is eased off, for it is old-fashioned,
a stigma easily explainable. Now,
we are free, we are liberated, we read philosophy;
we explore truth, pinned on the cardboard
we flutter our wings; pinned on the white, we speak black.
Now, let's have a bloodfest; now let us make a better world
while the universe crumbles.

A Village Shall Arrive...

The child stands at the door
his frail hand, the small fist
barely rises to knock; he can't–
shut out of the world, its warmth
he is only speechless. Raging inside
and yet there is no tear, there is nothing
but just the hand barely rising.

The afternoon stretches away, long hours
when the trees strew cool shade, the people drive by;
long hours of afternoon television, afternoon stocks
and soon.
there is no soon, for he's now sitting, he's asleep
at the doorway, and while dust rises, clouds form
there are dried eyes–eyes of the heart. There is nothing to show.

One little soul; one man. one does not count
as the world is busy; there is enough, and there is plenty
and one does not count. Days will come and go,
let him live with the hope of that door open; let him live
for who knows what's behind? They say, this is good
because who knows what's behind?
Let his nails claw the door open,
let him dig into it; let him eat the rotten wood.

They're happy, no pleased; they're pleased,
he's learning life, he will learn. Let him learn;
and they show their teeth, all thirty-two
they ruffle his hair in passing, they throw a glance
like he asked; as if he asked for that beggar's alms,
but they don't care, they like to give; and thus,
an afternoon goes by, a beautiful afternoon.

Let The Peacocks Dance

He wears white, he runs on a bicycle,
at traffic crossings he is in the middle
as either sides of him stream a crowd of dirty little fellows.
His laugh comes from his hands:
they make you happy of themselves;
soon the night falls, men are busy urinating
and at night halts they crush sugarcane at two am.
We cross the first bastion of the british, red and solid
without pretensions but to strike awe and fear, and we cross
the dirty stale rivers, while camphor rises up from the air
and in a land of rocks, the sea has yet to bite its teeth into
the cat is still doing his penance,
better to devour the mice and the birds.
Caught in the rituals, they want to defy gravity
and living in the paddy fields, they want to ask themselves
where does the new orleans join the madras
how the dark, nubile eyes, how the hearts skip beats
when we invent one. and all the world flows
as a few notes are born; flying scraps of will
like a patchwork quilt of colors, and let the world sing.
They cry, but unsure we keep moving
sitting at cape comorin, we try to hear the oceans, stories.

Door

The doorlight makes a cry into the night. The gaping hole of light is man's warmth, is man's habitation. It is man's death.

Untitled

Often,
a wind comes blows the sky away,
leaving holes in the trees
and songs in hearts.

But often,
the wind comes when men are asleep.

Feuilleton

From where do you peep, O cloud?
Men are asleep, like a cotton field,
were you to descend in a crash of fire
untouched will they be, for nothing have they to give you
but their shaky fears, whetted by the night breeze.

Go on, life, go where wild rivers rush to meet.
Here they burn like paper, with envy and admiration,
most of all, ambition. They rise and conquer cities,
master Word and seduce thoughts, they create grammars
for the flag to march down the aisle, the checkered floor.

Let the boy in this desert gaze after you, let him lose his hope.
He will die soon, for inside rust grows and tears gnaw,
like a curse, he will haunt yet not stay, accuse but not point;
the barren have their own maggots and birds of prey,
while they pretend to live, the gluttons multiply.

Density In The Matinee Show

The woman shrieks out loud, that's part of the repertoire,
she stuns the ears of the audience: "You can't do this!",
and a thud on the floor, all rise sobbing and clapping, heavy thud;
spectacles of death and tragedy, loss and gain. Mere fireworks.
The curtain's closing is always good; the lights are turned on.
Now, from a story in which one laughed and cried,
and believed to be in one,
now from that story,
like a flaming minaret shooting into the sky of halfdomes,
the man, the woman–the child,
propel; launch into dealing each other the double cards,
and keeping aces to yourself.
This is the show of life in which dramas come and go;
search for you and find a shadow on each wall;
the panoply of butterflies sticking to fruit,
or flies; search for life and meaning,
and find soul in every life, an instant of kiss;
your own, meet yourself.
The boy sits idly on the high wall,
with a penknife in his hand;
he scrapes every painting to know the makers' heart.
It's their heart he desires, not the art.

The Windows

stones flew–every drop of blood
crossed the roads, mixed in the gutters
and no one asked why. People
kept on passing, shops with happy awnings
kids remained playing; the dogs barked,
the sun beats down, with garlic and defecations
the perfume leaves a mark
on blue-tiled buildings, on the harbor where ships docked once,
on the messenger that feeds the pigeons everyday.

The Cynosure

In hushed black tones the inkwell speaks
to the night where angels hover,
From the last room's yellow light
I bounded out; soon
the talk dies, they are quiet,
accusing,
their fingers make a ring around me,
She sings
out the maggots that slumber,
the innocents left sleeping in cottonwool,
and now she stands on the center square,
a pedestal, an engraving, a veneration;
I crumble in decay, standing there weeping
but the tears do not water a single seed,
I burn up and the vision peters out
in the child playing on my dead chest, as red sun comes up.

Mezzanine

They tell me,
one door closes, another
opens.
But, till then
where to sojourn
in darkness, without a home
as if I were born
in a long corridor of brown doors
of a cheap hotel, cheap material.

They say,
don't think too much, wait,
forget for now,
but they do not know,
hope is memory now, desire is imagined
past; as if
I could have thought, when gnaw
hunger and numbness through my heart and mind
without lull or beginning.

Then I remember
a match in my hand
someone gave me scalding hot,
and when I open my fist
the scar eats up all my body,
only my mind remains
to light for another before I vanish,
for across this desert
only fire spreads wide and far.

How I Was Saved

I was late. The last metro, the last few weary glances seeped in tired self sarcasm. I sniggered, I felt a lump in my throat, I gazed ahead and felt the cold night hair slapping me as I stood at the open door. A day had fled by like a crow returning to its nest not yet satiated.

To burn a red fire while the world slept by, to laugh uncontrolled with the ghost sitting on that tree and watching me with bemused eyes was something I lived through the day for. He would come and lay claim to me one day, but he wanted one night of supineness from me, the cost of getting out from here. Till then I loved to stroke his hairless body, and enjoy the smile of evil anticipation, his and mine. We both were ghosts playing tictactoe.

I walked past the place where my father had said well if you don't stop crying we will leave you here alone. They well knew the fear of being alone, and hence they surrounded themselves in things that make them forget. And then among them I became alone and afraid. Would he like to eat me? I quickened my pace.

I come upon the banks of the Ganga; the newborn's head is shaved here, the ashes of the dead are floated here, an appropriate place I chuckled if this were the night. I looked in the muddy water, which was once glacier-fed and pure, now with the human touch and excreta, but man's object of reverence. I laughed out loud and loud, as if I were all the jackals who search for floating corpses. The mirror ripples, and the distorted face sets me running again.

I think I will try a labourer's sleep and drop outside a dirty slum where the smell of flesh pervades. It is warm here and I am almost in the grip of sleep, before I hear a woman's cry. Or maybe a laugh, I was too sleepy to determine. The mistless night carries sounds far, and I only hear the satisfaction gathered: perforce or not, does it matter? And I want to ask him, why me and not them, but he's not to be seen, the sly one. I run, I feel myself smelling.

I scan far and wide the whole country. Somewhere the girl was stoked in the brick kiln fire and I doubt she existed, since the world never knew her; he says he took her, but I even think she was his agent. I come upon men assembled; they talk a lot, spit a lot, talk a lot. And then laugh, but not happily. They laugh like it was a figure of speech, and they have a duty to make it happen. And they laugh and their bones shake, their bellies move, their eyes seem more limpid. They talk about creating markets and how more markets mean more development. It does seem reasonable; blind a man and he will develop acute hearing faculties. I wholeheartedly agree and clap. They throw me out; it was a polite gathering.

I move to a feast; they wipe bloods on their napkins and seem not to notice my smell. I feel welcome there, and make instant acquaintances with two half-dressed women with pearly teeth and faces upturned for the day. I ask him, these too?, he nods in silent enjoyment. I look at them very interested as prospective companions; their kind eyes don't do anything to deter me. But I begin to feel afraid: a live trophy, am I? I make a move.

I was early. On the lonely hill, only a vulture had its nest here. The sun would yet come up, and the keys winded, the clocks will start again, the toys will move again and babies will laugh, and the printing presses will run through the night. I sit down loosely, feeling his embrace tightening. And then I see the sun's first glimpse. I don't remember I was before here, and I see the circle slowly ascending, and I can trace the rays falling on the city prone. I can see the sap running up, every blade of grass quivering up, and man waking up to sun of own will, of own choice for once. More and more clear I can see her shape on the other side of the oceans, in another hemisphere; and the sun never sets.

I have never seen the ghost since that day.

PURPLE

The Return Of Life

For the drab newsprint staring out of the foggy morning corner
the sun's early. Just the tea smoke
rising, breaths locked and mixed, a foul night's efflux;
through the shining transparencies an eye of lust, an asana of yoga.
The candles didn't burn last night, and nor did
the stars glow; a boy cried on nobody's
shoulder and the sea shone brightly.
Now imagine the haystack smelling sweetly,
where men with bravado
come and deposit buxom girls and fall into their arms, their breasts,
where just a horse stands lonely and
the smell of pee mixes with cries of despair;
a twentyfour-hour's calling,
like they tugged hard at the mare before she died
crossing the vale,
a sky which shows up as mirror and not let the jasmine flower.
Sit on the rock, watch the sea waves lash
hear the songs of mollusks,
where does the blue end the green begin and why not
does the marine every moonlit night rise up to her lover? Hush,
the bandit will come and
take every newborn child out into the steppe,
the grass will be red of blood,
the sedges will rustle with deathcries for ever,
and no one will ask how did they come, who let them?

all will be forgotten
in pain and loss,
and soon the deserted townsquare will take upon a military march,
the beast within for the wild without. No!
The rain might come or not, the flower will choose to live
and find the lips to kiss her;
every patch of the earth rings with dances,
will hear a song. Dreams are aether; they float, they rise up.

Queues & Braids

I ask a cloud,
where is his tail?
He says, they don't have tails,
I refuse, I deny. to believe,
and I go further ahead, go ahead
and I meet a hillock with a lonely tree.
I ask the hillock,
where is his tail?
The hillock laughs, did he never hear a human voice
before? He says, he never had tail,
I refuse, I deny. to believe,
and I turn by a river, walk, walk
and I come upon a bee.
I ask her, where's her tail
and she disregards me, keeps buzzing
and when I persist, says she will bite me if I don't go
away. I refuse, deny to believe
and I curse the hive with hot mustard oil and go
to a very white bearded and matted sage. I wait
for he is meditating, and I wait several years,
he seems wise and I know I will get my answer
and I remain standing, remain. Then, one fullmoon night
the sage opens his eyes and without the question
says he never had a tail. I want to believe,
but I refuse, I deny. Heartbroken,
I start, before he asks me, "why are you looking?,
where is yours?"
I can only mutter, that is what I'm looking for,
where's mine that I never had.

Story ... Unfinished

The nebulous cap on his head, in a rainy late evening
when it's already dark and when the world is in the stages of life,
walks down the stone stairs; a few dogs prowl, a piazza waits empty,
the smell of bread where it wafts in the morning,
now only a few reeled bottles
and a sense of destiny.
It's funny how the inevitable winds up into everything,
like the moments attendant and watching; we call it fate,
we call it will.
The river is but a short mile away;
there he can smoke quietly and watch oneself
in quiet reflection of the red glimmer of
hope–whether live or stillborn, or pink
like a squealing baby,
ready to dance tarantulas and fling the best cloud on earth;
the moon's not yet quite there, and the buildings are hideous,
at most a woman on the corner,
or a student lost in sartre and making the world's riddles,
and there will be a step to sit, a joy to remember;
draw upon the painting,
there will be a canvas taut from one end to another:
a life lived and to come.

Still In The Wind

I sit in my window and watch the world below:
slow walks, marred by lost hopes, gouts and without purpose
waiting in the shuffling rain, under umbrellas grey and pink;
every often, a shriek comes,
from the town siren or a dog badly beaten
and wonder, where does the incense burn and go,
how many wreaths to count?

A few years back, the afternoon was bright and
the window was open,
and the birds sang.
The postman came and dropped mail in boxes painted shining,
there was tetris to play and a nice helicopter to make.
Real, circuitry.
Often I looked out and from the neighbour's radio arias floated out,
there were bright thieves with copper faces in every nook,
a city of twinkling glints.

I touch the frame, so dearly loved, so wooden for me,
my oldest association with teak, that wood that grows somewhere
where tigers are, where snakes live; I feel it, and know the smell,
I remember my mother's paints and I can still sense the varnish.
Brown longs for blue,
where birds return home and the cackle is still music.

They have given me names, some of love, rest of indifference–
to each name I have responded with
an identity of my own, one that
is in me, they not know; but, here,
when I see the black stripes melting with yellow
I feel all of them irrelevant. I hardly want to know, myself or them.
I want to plunge, straight into the golden light.
Oh yes, I still do dream.

and hope.

Sun Behind Me

Have you heard
in the profundity of night,
when a sliver of moon throws her hair down,
and sheds a red laugh,
a wolf's howl? A cry for lust, blood, food.

As I walk past the border, a guard
tight buttoned, half-sleeved, a bored face, a peaked cap
stop me: authority clashes with the inertia of my feet,
but that of my brain makes me stop–
do when you are ordered to.

Behind the sagebrush, old towns of murder sleep in,
and in the wakefulness of a restless soul the buttercups blight;
do you open the window and look for the silence? The sky
spreads like sieve, and music pours in, invisible to many.

I show my hands: they are empty, were always.
Except for a few lines
that no one knows to read, and a pulse beating at my wrist;
A hot wind borne from the plains faraway tosses my hair
so I know I am there, and while he checks the papers, I hope.

Snip, the sound of scissors. You love it, it makes a noise
it sits pretty, it kisses and leaves.

You work, the wheel turns round,
like precursor to great works,
to a laughter that spreads and reaches,
there, in the twinkle-lit corner,
you are; as the violet surrounds you.

Dry my hair, they are wet; fan me, make me sit and eat,
and let me know what springs from the earth here,
how tastes the water
and where do clouds rain;
the map shall remain folded in my breastpocket,
stained with the smell of my shirt, my pen,
and a heart's beat. Now untouched.

Inside The Alligator's Belly

to cook
humans delivered whole–
a frog croaks

too dark
a yawning of light
the next arrives

stone or rock
the boat hits
all over

Crossing

Years back I stood upon a ledge
never thought twice and crossed it,
I was but a child, and the dark
was empty, just black scowling visage.
Every marble played was one lost,
I was one of them, and I was happy
to find once again the silent fluid
running in my bones, and I was content.
But inexorable the urge was, and
a crack
peeled the plaster off walls of color,
soon I was but floating on winds of whim
and had I not taken sweet water with me
would've died of thirst in wide open sea.
The last crow had come onboard
when land was sighted, and benign skies
rained curses upon me, as I pushed the flag
in those vineyards where none had come
crossing the ocean; the host assembled,
arrived from back alleys, and fled before my march.

The Case Of A Little Piece Of $#@%

The star dropped a seed two years to this day.
Fell into a devout man's vessel of worship,
and unaware if God's blessing or Other's temptation
the man read an incantation, and gave it as alms.
The beggar was blind but not without nose,
and sensing a chance, he tried to play the magician:
drop a coin, and see what happens!
Many came, and many were fooled, since ready to believe,
and many came, and were not amused, since ready to scorn,
but both were good for the beggar, and now installed
he was the Holy Man. From far and wide came budding politicians,
men with two wives, women with no sons,
and farmers with no harvest,
all returned a bit happier. For some,
it worked; for some, it still didn't,
and then when it didn't
a few grumbled, cursed their fate, and went again to the Holy Man.
Thus wide and far grew a new following,
and every evening they gathered to hear him, to watch him.
And an evening came, when the star again dropped,
but this time on the Holy Man's well shaven head:
and now behold the wrath, the cheatedness! In a swarm
they came and attacked him, and left not a bone untouched:
the indication, they shouted, The Indication!
It can't be wrong, The Indication.

Moonshine

the owls
fly. goblins
in rice baskets
glimmer, sing
shine.
like stars, in
rangolis at dawn. but
washed
dogs
grumble.
no one sleeps;
all murmur
or snore.
no one winks.

The True Story Remembered In A Dream

The King had cried and cried for five hours. No, the barber wasn't amused;
the hair got sticky and he also snivelled a lot, let out lot of mucus,
a sticky beard is a daunting proposition, and every hair was silken and white
and a pride of the forty ministers and the forty dominions all round;
And yet now the night was coming, a fresh maiden from the harem shall wait his pleasure,
like well oiled black boots he must be made young; and the chase should smell blood, blood.

News broke out then, the tiger from Siam–they had imported one newly,
was mauling the new Queen and was on the way to the King's chamber;
the retainers fled, and the barber thought here is the way to win his way to the King's heart
and his beard–for now the King was white and unmoving, blanched more than the muslin curtains billowing;
He proposed, "It is not a big concern, Your Majesty; the tiger is but desirous to see me,

if you wish the way from Her Majesty's palace is long, and you may hear the tale."

The King could only nod, whether of a desire to hear or only a tremble none could ever say,
and forthwith: "Now as Your Worship might know more well than me, the land is full of
vipers and trees that suck children out of mothers' laps; of white-fanged dragons and an air full of yellow diseases,"
Here, it might be remarked that the King looked round, to verify the atmosphere, and his skin being yet shrivelled and white,
he again listened half ready to die, "and once as a ship barber I gone to this land, ready armed with my razor so none could trouble me;
there find you the best business, Your Mighty Highness, for they know not hair are meant to cut and make handsome, and even a woman is of service to me. Now...

"I had made a mighty fortune there, till one day the Governor there heard me of, and he sent for me
in all curiosity to ogle at a man not a native and not a white man, and with a box of scents and lathers and charms and a hand ready to slit a throat,
and that was a day I never can regret enough." The King was now curious about this other ruler, and the barber knew now the pride is pricked,
"A short man am I, Your Lordship, and not a man who carries his arms in his muscles or in his brains, not even in his firearms
and having listened of my powers from all quarters, he no less expected a giant of six feet, lording with lionskins on his shoulders and a mace or a gun to carry;
But I see my work well enough where it is needed, and there was the man with a face not washed since he was a babe and a beard so hard as–well, let me show you–"

The barber then worked up a tornado of foam on the King's beard and let it drip down easy enough, and started being busy with the razor, very
busy as if his best work were to come; "Well, this was how I sized him up, Your Magnificence, and I knew in a second the man's hairs only show up hard and obstinate; but once the soap touched them, they were falling like village belles for a soldier from victory...,"
—a roar, another—the silence of the palace, and the tiger coming closer, the King cries, "What are you doing, you fool? I thought you were to tell me
how to tame the tiger! Quick, do something, all your tricks you learnt, stop the maneater!" The barber, "Yes, Sire," and no better time than this,
he worked the foam and slit the King's throat, a dying booty for the tiger to taste but still warm.

Forty days later, the young Prince without a hair was on the throne, and the royal barber had not a work to do for all the rest of his life but tell tales of Siam—to the Prince.

RED

Forefinger; Fist; Palm

Here I stand with a book in my hand
a small square window high away,
a sparrow somewhere in the sky
and here I stand in the middle,
in the prison where they locked me.
Rustle of sharp teeth, the gnawing of hunger
and a world where orange has turned white,
and all wear dappled suits,
but within, a darkness.
The night that makes me forget the day,
makes me want to forget the day.
Because here I live, in this prison where they locked me.

Ideas come to me, new and strangely beautiful,
of a dancing girl
with *patins*, with arms flowing like wings;
and in the applause and in the silence
in the sweat she feels and in the love
that throbs alone in her breast,
there is but the fertility of trees,
the anger of joy left nude. They survive,
and fill these grey walls of somber chants
with laughter of performance
sobs of inability, gasps of struggles; they survive,
and here I stand in the prison with old friends met today.

There are cool, dark lairs, that you sybarite may love;
there is the music
that permeates and eats up me
the one where thoughts flit and fly, incoherent but
making the shape known,
their shadows flying like angels hovering above me;
Everywhere light travels,
and makes the time known; but here where I stand
time marks its own stoppage,
like a broken spindle rolling and rolling, in chaste faithfulness,
and just a password, a name,
and some food passed to me, my rations where they locked me.

The keys might have rusted long since,
and I cannot pray; but when the moon comes up
I hear the moths crumble,
I make love to the insects that bite my lips,
and I know I exist, I will still live.
Though they may lock me here
my pleasures remain, my deeds remain.
The choices are theirs to give
but the moments are mine to take,
and this is where they lost, this is how.
I might be the one who destroys,
but I have my love to give. Let me dream

of a song of the sparrows. It's been a long time.

Where Nest Is

I wonder where crows, black as ravens, fly to
In this frozen land, with hardly a warm nook,
Where they build their nests, how they rear their young.

The man says, he don't know,
But then points to a clump of deodars,
Tall and immovable, standing like sentinels of time,
Or to an eye that can straddle space and ages,
Waymarkers of the valley, of the songs,
And says–

Maybe there,
For even at its thickest, when all else is buried deep
Under snow, the trunk of deodar shall have no ice clinging,
Intact, it will keep offering warmth, like
A beautiful story, a true heart.

Where Nesting Is

Breaths of Tea and loud guffaws mingle,
Like Honey in water, Ginger everywhere;
There's a Gun-Man wanted somewhere,
Over which riverbank to patrol, I wonder.
Who are the intruders in this innocent land?
Snow and rain have long ceased to be regarded,
As a matter of fact, avalanches come
And before going leave a newsitem in wake;
However I watch the stars on the hillside
Dotting after dusk the human presence,
What outlasts is five o'clock in the morning
When a dimly-lit bus station waits as beacon.
Only from afar; for inside there is a
Woman sleeping on her lover's shoulder,
A TV playing crime news, and already commence
Hoarse cries of bus conductors, not
Seeking passengers, but the joy of being awake
In early, early morning.

Where Birds Are

In the middle of snowdrift,
A tiny hamlet stands, its little fires
Making no more noise than birds to the scanning passenger;
It remains, as if born with the rocks,
with the river's sharp, snakelike thunder,
And decays, as if with the harness of dams,
as the water trickled, so did life ebb.

I am standing on the opposite brow,
A few hundred metres of chasm is all in between;
Keen night air whips about my face,
Brings faint color to cheeks otherwise sallow,
As I watch with bated breath life
Coming alive in the dark universe.

One, two, five and seven, I count the lights
Of a house or barn, or maybe one old family
Now respected by a dozen progenitors;
The stars bloom one by one,
And ere I turn to bed, shall keep talking
In holy converse with those above.

The Song Of The Angels

The night
often wakes me up,
cold fingers, searching for warmth,
like death pleading for life.
At those times I cough, I put on a warm shawl,
and while the milk comes to a slow boil
I count the glow worms, and see if they are more
than my pulse beats.
I hate them when they shine for the moon and the river,
everywhere in the low grasses, coveting the fickle shine
that won't last two weeks; while here I,
I await them for stories to hear, for them to kiss my breasts.

The nights of darkness, they shine and gather around me
stringing on my golden hair, making a necklace to adorn me
they say how far they come from, how long one night is;
from India and Ceylon, where the tigers meditate
and the elephants rumble, those living lives
of the bazaars of Dacca and the old port of Calicut,
the stars gather, and the eyelashes droop
and I wonder, I laugh, I cry. I tell them this must be false,
where did they, mere fireflies, get such rhapsodies from?

And one night, a firefly, wizened and small and hardly a light,
descended on me from Siberia; and I was not to know

the night I fell in love. She told me
of Vytrytva[1], the man who lived maybe a few centuries ago
who became strong by the night and slept idle by the day;
a silent sufferer, I wondered where his power came from?
The stones he lifted all night up the mountain,
or the silence and the contempt he belaboured in, useless
when the others worked, a man bulging for no reason?

Others are prisoners of their minds and their wills,
while I am of my own body; like night's silence
my silence will have various names;
anger and dark, bottomless and death;
who will hear the slinking panther,
the trespasser stealing for bread, or the sun
silently gaining ground? Who will hear the dying
wings of those who make light while yet there is plague?
Not many, but those who will
will own the earth, and unsheathed shall their words drip,
like blood and fire. With love and poetry.

[1]Hero from a Chukchi folktale

Elegies

Eyelids flutter, they wake up, fall down, tremble,
A grin, a beauty, a dance of light; isn't it, the moment
a truth? Where shall I seek yet more divinity; which absolute
that stays and rots, where does the remaining stench add up to?

The sea whispers, the thousand porpoises that play and bounce,
the prattle and the conversation, the silence and the meaning,
and the unmeaning. The laugh born of pleasure, or habit; the new
born rabbit's son, the fawn in a forest nude and green.

Drop of water that beams upon me from the blue sky,
the dog's tail
that curlily, very roundedly goes past me,
the hungry dog with a hanging
tongue, a jaw that has tasted nothing; here and there the bell rings,
here and there people descend and arrive;
and here the sun is, here the rain.

Bring the red butter, bring the purple butter;
the night spent in greasing pans,
reading books, making paper camels;
the morning three o'clocks spent shaving,
reading out aloud the crudest jokes,
the most serious poetry; outside,
a piteous wind howls, a dark winter threatens;
but the stars shall twinkle, burst.

Galleries Under The Earth

You give me a book, I say, "Where
What do I read?" The answer's in your eyes,
and I look for it in the book. And I ask, "Where?"
Rain comes and goes; and lights dim and glow,
people on the busy shopping streets, the hubbub,
strong perfumes,
and I walk around with the book in my hand, stopping
at every traffic post and in every joint.
They point all at the book.

The dust-jacket is torn, the contents pages are missing
and I already read the preface and the end: somewhere
I find a bookmark, of maple leaf, now skeleton
and I smell it, taste it, bite it; the essence
is it there? I do not know, and I look at you
but not your eyes; I only look for indications–
your motions, your nods, something I know to read.

I fling it to the corners which spiders share
and hope them to unravel it for me; answers
ready-made, tailor-made–and while I torture
the paint goes green, the sky falls down around me
and one by one the idols crack, slowly the earth sunders;
only the book remains, now moth-eaten,
with dusty webs entangled
and I ask, "Whose book is it? Why?"

I remember, whose; I drop the book and set out,
but a cold wind takes me, stars extinguishing wherever I look up,
in the darkness I walk: I know not where to you, but I walk.

Bookmarker

Through several Guignols[1] I travelled through,
sometime a shining gold tooth newly filled in, also
the green cape, or the warm smell of punch newly minted;
rarely I was also the nudge and tired titter, the yellow eye
out of its corner,
wolfing newly designed women with sheeplike pouts.

But once I was a leaf,
a maple leaf that swirled and whirled in the thick winter wind,
something made to trample when the show closes and all go home.
A thickly veined being like me, heavy with its own body
yet aspires to flecked ceilings;
a ware neither of songs nor clattering
laughter, like plain old cracked piece of *argile*,
I still dream to dare drop down
chimneys of shining embers and porridge,
and to adorn something other than flags and crowns;

To be kissed by your lips once,
and kept in your notebook of poems.

[1]French puppet shows, with the main character representing silk industry workers.

Elopement

I held her hands,
warm in henna, when
all lights went off.

By The Water

When the last kiss was exchanged,
the evening was burning away, laughter was still in the ears,
with the lonely spire the mute witness,
a big bell to translate the day's mourning,
there were hardly riverbanks left where they had not walked;
amidst these well-trodden corners, often a breath arose
not in prayer, nor in murmur of love; neither in vain glory,
but what goes by sigh. Nor the moan, neither the grunt,
but the clasp of a brooch, a sound with a fulfilment beneath,
and opening under.

In Your Heart, Valise, I Be

To bring the silence, first light a match, shade the light,
cup your palms, and then when the flame's steady
let it glow, let it burn. Let the light be.

One, two, the water boiling on a woodfire spills over,
a fire whose smoke rises and spreads joy, perfume;
and calling me her own, yours; the smile takes on
disguises, and new faces, as I run, run
to the last acre of sky for some more stars; our feast.

Impending Ruin

The winter has come early,
My foot had stuck in the mud last evening;
I was not mindful,
thinking of the work yet to be done,
her happy smile, waiting glance
of expectancy was not new, I brushed it aside
and soon settled into a creased forehead and warm
cup of tea, all my own;
now I face the frost left by the night dew,
and I look for hope on her face, now
without fight, I seek inspiration.

Summer was fast one day, when I had gone
to the crossing; seldom did master go
to bring home his revenues from that wild place,
and object of envy and attention, I had liked the place,
after all the hardships, it greeted me warm.
Soon weary of life I found a girl who sparkled,
her eyes took me to the sea I dreamt of when young
though they had yet to become deep; soon before I knew,
I had got myself a happy home, a heated rug.
She yielded everything without question;
this troubled me first, but soon habit grew, and the year passed.

Sitting now with only will of God to wait for
and the opened books staring at me
from the window of next year's
autumn, I wait for the questions to gather, to bring one blast
in fury, where leaves swirl at the portico and do not leave,
remain standing, remain seated, not knowing to turn or not.
Not made to ask,
yet as the winds race in the last corners of sunlight,
I know, her every breath taken is a curse on me,
my accursed creed;
unmindful, is she less or does she not belong; or like
a jackal I leave the tasted meat to return to in famine,
while I seek pleasures of salted rot in stalls all around?
The books are heavy, I alone carry them.

Love Is Blue

Blinded in his tears and the flying dust
as the dark day creeps up the fat, sleeping, suave men,
He swings the hammer at the stake in the ground, he swings
and watches his large muscles grinding down an insignificant
marker to his life. The clouds break sometimes,
to show him the map where no one will tread,
the line that is drawn.

He will meet me at the station outside the rainbow
where lorries stand in long queues for gasoline, where
the savannah has vanished from and only bright scarfs flutter;
There we shall loiter and laugh for our penny-pinched dollops,
and it is there I will know his hands, gentle but rough
with scalded veins, with nothing written in them but misery.

Soon the flailing snows shall drive us from the barren grassland
where we chose to be adventurous,
and our retreat will be a monastery;
shaved heads will look at him curiously,
rarely a man handsome comes there,
but my one wonder will be, does the brave need to pray?
Where does one search for oneself:
amidst the throng, or in the silent gnawing
night, when alone with conscience and deeds,
when there is no one to plead with.

I look at him, the next day while we are going back
to the town of peat and smoke,
and I put a hand on his shoulder, his forehead:
I feel his trembling of within.
No, you did not do this? He can only look,
he can only know
the protest of my words, the ardent zeal in my eyes.
As the gnarled trees embrace,
so do we in our wretchedness; shadows cross our distorted faces,
but do we care? All we know is our hands in one another,
and our whim to live.

Bridge Over The Seine

Red ice, sparkling ice
and boys play everywhere,
in the onslaught
and in the stampede of laughter,
in that mass swirling on the Seine;
as masks jostle, red lips burst
and in winter's blackness
born of the heart's white barrenness
are words traded, glances exchanged
and warm hands held; but one day,

the winter shall go away. The seed is
a tree, and wind and water shall be at
his own seeking;
frozen lakes will be the pools of joy
forgotten, and we will be studying
how birds migrate back.

But in the land of the desert
there are no seasons; and all you and I can do
is to live those times in our heads.
And wait, yea adamantly wait
that rains come to our parched lands
snows fall thick on our doorsteps
and without the judgement, beyond the measuring up
there be only eyes that shower love.

That day, we will cross the seven seas
meet the Nenets, drink the burgundy, and lie like cormorants,
and the bridge will once again be full
of stories peopled by our thoughts,
and thoughts peopled by our stories.
That day, on the beautiful arch of seven colors, we may kiss.

The Abode Of God

In homes of little mice
We live,
In pawprints of little rabbits
We walk,
Ask me where do you live,
I shall say, in my smell,
And you will say, in my longing.

Our homes are not built of mud or brick,
Nor of tiles, iron or glass;
We have no homes, the expelled, the exiled.
The Moon suckles us to her breast,
And as we make love, a tear rolls down, shining
Like the pearls which are my presents to you:
A solemn gift, a marriage gift.

You will not know where to stop,
And neither will I where to begin,
We are the unceasing, the cycle of this universe,
Time is our home, the lap in which we sleep
As seasons, we wane and wax, but remain strong,
Bountiful in our joyous loving,
Irreverent in our morality.

Far And Near, Near And Far

Word comes.
Like mosquito bite,
auguring rains, monsoon, dinning tin
of the roof, milling frogs sin.

Drips slowly, like lemon drops in honey,
News of arrival; news of being,
News of rivers in spate, of a world washed
with Hands of destiny, of love mashed

like Potatoes. Boiled in the cooker,
and fried with pepper and oil and appetite,
As rain falls, life comes alive, in within,
The whistle sings, and the Word lives in.